W9-BDF-464

BREAD
MACHINE
Magic
& More

AMERICAN
★COOKING★
GUILD™

Boynton Beach, Florida

Acknowledgments
—Cover Design and Layout by Pearl & Associates, Inc.
—Cover Photograph and styling by Burwell & Burwell
—Back cover photo by Rebecca Wicks, Wix Pix Productions
—Illustrations by Jim Haynes, Graphics Plus

Revised Edition 1997

More...Quick Recipes for Creative Cooking!
The American Cooking Guild's *Collector's Series* includes over 30 popular cooking topics such as Barbeque, Breakfast & Brunches, Chicken, Cookies, Hors d' Oeuvres, Seafood, Tea, Coffee, Pasta, Pizza, Salads Italian and many more. Each book contains more than 50 selected recipes. For a catalog of these and many other full sized cookbooks, send $1 to the address below and a coupon will be included for $1 off your first order.

Cookbooks Make Great Premiums!
The American Cooking Guild has been the premier publisher of private label and custom cookbooks since 1981. Retailers, manufacturers, and food companies have all chosen The American Cooking Guild to publish their premium and promotional cookbooks. For further information on our special markets programs please contact the address.

The American Cooking Guild
3600-K South Congress Avenue
Boynton Beach, FL 33426

Table of Contents

INTRODUCTION

My wife taught me how to bake bread years ago, and we've been doing it ever since. We bake our own bread not because we love to bake, but because we love to eat good bread—and most readily available bread is awful.

We are not gadget lovers—we still don't have a food processor. But because of time, and one thing or another, we were too busy to bake bread as often as we'd like. We had heard glowing reports about the new automatic breadmakers, and that what came out of them was terrific. So we bought a bread machine.

It took maybe two days to discover the potential of the thing, and another two days to discover that many of the recipes that came with the machine could be improved upon. My wife and I began developing recipes of our own, drawing from our years of bread baking experience. This book is the end result.

The recipes were developed in our kitchen, in our own breadmakers (we ended up with two of them). These are the recipes we use most. They have been tested by us, our family and our neighbors in regular kitchens—not high tech corporate kitchens full of home economists. Further, the ingredients are off the shelves of local grocery stores. The recipes work in all the regular sized (one pound) and the larger (one and a half pound) bread machines presently sold.

You see, you don't really need a big, expensive cookbook with hundreds of recipes and fancy four color photographs just to make bread. This little book and your imagination should just about do it. Have fun!

ABOUT BREAD MACHINES

Automatic breadmakers are simple to use. You measure out all the ingredients according to your recipe, load the bread pan and press the start button. The machine mixes the ingredients, and provides the right temperatures and timing for rising and baking. Several hours later, a beeper sounds and the bread or dough is finished.

There are dozens of different bread machines on the market. They tend to be square (except for the big Welbilt, which is round), weigh 15 pounds, more or less, sit on the kitchen counter and use regular household current. Each unit has a bread pan with a handle and a kneading blade that fits in the bread pan. Some machines have a yeast dispenser, while others instruct you to add the yeast with the other ingredients. Capacity varies. Some breadmakers produce 1-pound loaves about 7 inches long, 5 inches in diameter, yielding 8 to 10 slices of bread. The larger machines produce 1½-pound loaves that are 9 inches long, 6½ inches in diameter, yielding 12 slices of bread.

Before you start to use this book you should be familiar with your bread machine. Read the owner's manual thoroughly. You should also bake a few loaves of bread in the machine using the recipes provided by the manufacturer, just to give you a feel for your machine and how it operates.

While each recipe in this book provides the ingredients list and general instructions, you'll need to follow the basic guidelines and directions for your machine for baking the loaves.

We have verified the recipes in the two types of machines—those that add the yeast automatically and those in which you add the yeast with the rest of the ingredients. The recipes in this book work in both types of machines and there isn't a noticeable difference in the final result.

Some bread machines have timers that allow you to combine the ingredients and program the machine to start at a later time. This can be a fun option if you enjoy waking up to the smell of a freshly baked breakfast loaf. If you use the timer, be sure to bake breads that call for ingredients that won't easily spoil if left at room temperature for hours.

While breadmakers are user friendly and rather forgiving, you may find that you will have to make minor adjustments in some of the recipes—a little more or less water or flour for instance, to adapt them to your particular machine.

There is also the time of year to consider, the ambient temperature, the humidity and the climate in general. All can have an effect on your loaves.

One cold winter, we and our neighbors began to think there was something wrong with our machines—the bread wasn't rising as high as usual. Among other things, the tap water was scarcely above 32°. The machines didn't like that. I ended up making my bread on the dough cycle, letting it rise in a warmed-up oven, with the light on, then baking it in the oven. The results were wonderful.

THE DOUGH SETTING

After enjoying the ease of homemade bread from our machine we began trying the recipes using the *dough mode*. We use this dough setting as much, or more, than the bake setting.

On the dough mode, the machine mixes ingredients, kneads the dough and allows it to rise. Then, you remove the dough from the bread pan, shape it, give it a final rising and bake in a conventional oven. The dough mode allows you to bake lots of things besides traditional loaves—long baguettes, skinny bread sticks, fluffy rolls, gooey cinnamon buns, crispy pizza dough and more.

If you don't have a dough setting, you can still use the machine for making the dough. Simply load the bread pan as usual, then remove the dough after about 1½ hours.

The dough setting helps you time your dough preparation accurately. It also makes it possible to prepare dough the night before, put it in the refrigerator overnight, and finish up the baking in time for breakfast. Early morning baking is something most people don't do—unless they happen to like getting up at four in the morning.

DAVE'S PIZZA TRICK

For a crispier pizza crust, make your pizza dough (page 63) early in the day and leave it to rise for several hours in the fridge. This was discovered by our neighbor, Dave Parry. He teaches Philosophy at Penn State, so you know he's smart.

BAKING BREAD BY HAND

These recipes can be baked out of the machine, if you prefer. Your kitchen should be 70° to 80° and draft-free. Here's how:

Pour ¼ cup very warm water (120°) into a large bowl. Add yeast, stirring to dissolve. Mix in remaining water, other liquids, butter or oil, salt, sugar or honey, stirring until smooth. Mix in ⅓ of the flour and other dry ingredients, by hand or with a mixer (use dough hooks if your mixer has them). Mix for a few minutes, add the next ⅓ of the flour and mix again. Add final ⅓ of the flour and mix until the dough is smooth and elastic, yet stiff.

Turn dough out onto a floured surface. Knead the dough for 10 minutes. Place dough into a greased bowl, turning it over so the top is coated with oil. Cover and place in a warm draft-free spot. Let dough rise until double in size, about one hour. Remove dough from bowl and punch it down. Shape and place into greased loaf pans or on greased baking sheets. Cover and let rise until doubled, about 45 minutes. Bake in a preheated 350° oven until brown, 40 to 50 minutes. Remove loaves from pans and place on a wire rack to cool.

HOW TO KNEAD BREAD DOUGH

Kneading determines the texture of the finished loaf—whether it is tender or coarse. To knead, place dough on a floured surface. Push your hands into the dough to press out the air. Give dough a quarter turn, then fold in half and press flat. If dough is sticky, sprinkle with flour. If it is dry, sprinkle with water. Continue folding and flattening, kneading about 10 minutes total.

THE INGREDIENTS

Yeast:
Along with flour and water, yeast is the foremost ingredient in bread. Yeast is a microscopic plant or fungus that helps turn sugar into alcohol. This process makes a gas. As the gas expands it makes the dough rise. If your dough isn't rising, old yeast may be the culprit. All the recipes in this book call for regular dry yeast. If you use Rapid Rise, Instant or Breadmaker Yeast, adjust the quantity according to package directions.

Flour:
Bread machine manufacturers recommend bread flour. It is milled from hard winter wheats which are high in protein. It is expensive and we've found that unbleached all-purpose flour, which is a mixture of soft and hard wheats, works well in bread machines. It's cheaper and the bread has a nicer texture.

High Gluten Flour:
Unbleached white flour, with the fats and sugars rinsed off, is high in protein and produces a rich, dense, somewhat coarse crumb. You can add high gluten flour to all purpose or whole wheat flour to help it rise.

Whole Wheat Flour:
This is flour with the whole kernel of the wheat milled in. It has to be handled a little differently. The whole kernels inhibit the development of gluten in the bread dough. Many breadmakers have a Whole Wheat setting that gives the dough a little more time to work and rise. We often throw in a tablespoon or two of whole wheat flour in with our regular white bread dough for extra flavor and nutrition.

Other Flours:
There are other flours besides wheat—rye potato flour, rice and soy. There are also the coarser flours such as cornmeal, oatmeal, pumpernickel, graham or bran. You can use these in your breadmaker but they should be used in combination with the bread or all purpose flour.

Liquids:
In baking, liquids bind the other ingredients together. Water works best, but in a fit of inspiration you can try other things. Milk gives a denser crumb and more nutrition. It is used in many sweet dough recipes. Dry milk has less fat and is easy to work with. Fruit juice, with its extra natural sugar, enhances the working of the yeast. One liquid we use often is potato water. Save the water drained off after boiling potatoes and keep it in the refrigerator. It is invaluable in making good sour dough rye.

Salt:
The salt strengthens the gluten structure and restricts the development of the yeast. It also enhances flavor—you don't want to make bread without it. Add one teaspoon per 2½ cups of flour.

Sweeteners:
Sugar or other sweeteners feed the yeast and act as a preservative. We often use honey or brown sugar. Molasses is good for raisin, anadama and dark rye bread.

Shortening:
The shortening makes dough easier to work with and makes for a smoother texture and a tender, dense crumb. It also acts as a preservative. Butter does wonderful things for bread's flavor and texture. Lard is absorbed by hard wheat flour even better. It makes an even more tender crumb and crust, is easy for the stomach to digest, and leaves virtually no residual flavor. You can use vegetable shortening. A little bacon fat does wonders in rye. Oils, especially olive oil, do all of the above and add that rich savory flavor that distinguishes Italian bread and pizza dough.

Other Ingredients:
Fruits, nuts, cheese, vegetables—you can use them all. These added ingredients tend to inhibit dough rising, so the final product may be flat or a bit sunken on the top, but the bread will taste wonderful. Usually you have to add a little more yeast. Also you may want to try toasted bread crumbs in some of your rye breads to enrich the flavor. Place a quarter of a cup of bread crumbs on a cookie sheet under your broiler just until brown. Add to rye or pumpernickel bread.

A SHOPPING LIST

Here's a short shopping list of things bakers will want to have around the kitchen. None of the ingredients are expensive and all are readily available. If you plan to bake a lot of bread, check around for the best prices.

Flour
We rarely buy flour in bulk— meaning 10 to 25 pound sacks. It is just as cheap to buy the handy five pound bags (we may buy ten of them when they are on sale). Flour will last up to two years when kept nicely wrapped. You'll get seven loaves from a five pound bag with the regular sized bread maker, and about four to five with the large.

High Gluten Flour
Buy a pound or two of it. You can strengthen your all purpose, unbleached all purpose, or whole wheat flour by adding a tablespoon or two of high gluten flour to it.

Yeast
Plan to buy yeast in bulk—it is much less expensive. We buy our yeast in one pound bags, keep several ounces in a jar in the fridge, and the rest wrapped tightly in the freezer. We use about a pound of yeast every three months.

Non-Fat Dry Milk
Some recipes call for non-fat dry milk. If you are out of it, add a couple of ounces of whole milk to the water in the recipe.

Lard
Flour absorbs lard better than other shortening, creating a bread with a nice soft texture. You only use a tablespoon or less at a time, so you shouldn't have to worry about being reported to the food police. A one pound package costs less than a dollar and you find it in your grocer's meat case. Kept tightly wrapped, it will last for a month or two.

Unsalted Butter

This is the best shortening, next to lard. Store it in the freezer if you don't use a lot of it. If you are still nervous about cholesterol levels, margarine works well in place of lard or butter.

Spices

Cinnamon, of course, and mace or nutmeg, and cardamom are delicious in bread. Store brands are often just as good as the "leading brands" and are less expensive.

Liqueurs

Triple Sec, Amaretto, or Banana Liqueurs are a good way to add flavor both to dough and flavored butters. I buy the miniature bottles of the less expensive brands and these work fine.

Other Supplies to Have On Hand:

Baguette pans
Candied citrus rind (orange or lemon)
Marble rolling pin
Raisins

Mail Order:

King Arthur is a mail-order company that specializes in baking supplies including bread pans, flours, yeast and flavorings. Write or call for their catalog if you can't find what you need in your area:

King Arthur Flour Baker's Catalogue

P.O. Box 876
Norwich, Vermont 05055-0876
(800) 827-6836

Chapter 1

Very Basic Machine Made Breads

REAL BASIC BREAD

This is as basic as bread can be. It is ideal for those conscious about diets, fat, cholesterol and the like. It doesn't keep well, so eat it promptly or use any leftover slightly stale bread for French toast.

REGULAR
⅞ cup water
2¼ cups bread flour
1 tsp salt
1½ tsps yeast

LARGE
1⅛ cups water
3 cups bread flour
1¼ tsps salt
2 tsps yeast

Fill the bread pan and bake according to the instructions for your machine.

Yield: 1 loaf

FRENCH TOAST

There are as many recipes for French Toast as there are Frenchmen. This is a delicious way to get rid of stale bread.

1 egg, beaten
½ cup light cream
4 slices stale bread
1 stick butter
confectioners sugar, as garnish

Combine beaten egg and cream. Dip slices of bread into egg mixture, turning to coat both sides. Melt butter in a skillet over medium heat. Add dipped bread to skillet and sauté until golden. Turn and sauté on second side.

When done, remove French toast from pan and dust with confectioners sugar. **Yield:** 2 servings.

BASIC WHITE BREAD

This is your standby white bread. Vary it by adding more or less sugar or butter—better yet, substitute a teaspoon of lard for the butter. When you get the recipe just the way you like it, commit it to memory or write it on an index card and slip it under your bread machine.

REGULAR

2¼ cups bread flour
¼ cup milk
⅝ cup water
1 tsp salt
1 Tbsp sugar
1 tsp butter or lard
1½ tsps yeast

LARGE

3 cups bread flour
⅓ cup milk
⅞ cup water
1¼ tsps salt
1½ Tbsps sugar
1½ tsps butter
2 tsps yeast

Load the bread pan and bake according to the instructions for your machine.

Yield: 1 loaf

PENNSYLVANIA MAID SYRUP

Once you make your own pancake, waffle or French toast syrup, you'll never use store-bought syrup again.

2 cups sugar
1 cup water
⅓ cup pure (uncut) maple syrup*

Bring sugar and water to a boil. Cook for a few minutes, until syrup is clear. Then add maple syrup and cool. Store in a tightly covered jar.

*or ½ tsp maple flavoring plus ½ tsp vanilla extract
Yield: 2 cups syrup

WHOLE WHEAT BREAD

This basic wheat bread makes delicious toast. If your bread machine has a whole wheat cycle, be sure to use it.

REGULAR

1¾ cups bread flour

½ cup whole wheat flour

¼ cup milk

⅝ cup water

1½ Tbsps brown sugar

1 Tbsp butter

1 tsp salt

1½ tsps yeast

LARGE

2¼ cups bread flour

¾ cup whole wheat flour

⅓ cup milk

⅞ cup water

2 Tbsps brown sugar

1½ Tbsps butter

1½ tsps salt

2 tsps yeast

Load the bread pan and bake according to the instructions for your machine.

Yield: 1 loaf

CROUTONS

Don't throw away that slightly stale bread—make croutons! These are delicious as a topping for soups or salads.

sliced bread, slightly stale

olive oil

herbs, parmesan cheese, salt & pepper, to taste

Cut sliced bread into cubes. Heat olive oil in a heavy skillet. Add dried herbs if desired. Add bread cubes to oil, and cook until they begin to brown, stirring frequently so they don't burn. Remove from pan with slotted spoon to paper towels. Dust with parmesan cheese, salt and pepper to taste.

BASIC RYE BREAD

To me, rye bread is not so much basic as it is essential. If your machine has a rye setting, be sure to use it.

REGULAR

1¾ cups bread flour
½ cup rye flour
⅞ cup water
1½ Tbsps brown sugar
1 Tbsp olive oil
1½ tsps salt
2 tsps caraway seeds
1½ tsps yeast

LARGE

2¼ cups bread flour
¾ cup rye flour
1⅛ cups water
2 Tbsps brown sugar
1½ Tbsps olive oil
2 tsps salt
1 Tbsp caraway seeds
2 tsps yeast

Load the bread pan and bake according to the instructions for your machine.

Yield: 1 loaf

RON'S GOOEY DOUGH HINT

If your dough is wet and gooey, you might think there is a mistake in the recipe. The answer is probably the flour. While manufacturers try to keep their flour consistent, wheat is a plant. The solution for wet dough is simple: work a little more flour into it, let it rest 5 minutes, then go on with the recipe. My brother-in-law, Ron Kurtz, looks inside his bread machine about 10 minutes after starting it. If the dough looks wet, he throws in a couple of tablespoons of flour.

Chapter 2

Dark, Rye and Whole Grain Breads

GOOD WHOLE WHEAT BREAD

You can substitute brown sugar for the molasses, if you prefer.

REGULAR	LARGE
1¼ cups bread flour	2 cups bread flour
1 cup whole wheat flour	1 cup whole wheat flour
⅝ cup water	¾ cup water
¼ cup milk	½ cup milk
1 Tbsp molasses	1½ Tbsps molasses
1 Tbsp butter	1½ Tbsps butter
1 tsp salt	1½ tsps salt
1½ tsps yeast	2 tsps yeast

Load the bread pan and bake according to the instructions for your machine.

Yield: 1 loaf

BREAD PUDDING

Rich and old-fashioned, you'll savor every bite.

4 cups milk	3 eggs
3 cups cubed bread	1 tsp vanilla
¼ cup butter	juice of ½ lemon
½ cup sugar	2 Tbsps Gran Marnier
½ tsp salt	or triple sec liqueur
grated rind of ½ lemon	½ cup raisins

Scald milk in a saucepan. Pour into a large glass bowl. Add the bread cubes, butter, sugar, salt, lemon zest. Stir to combine. In a small bowl, beat eggs. Add vanilla, lemon juice and liqueur. Add egg mixture to bread mixture. Stir in raisins. Place glass bowl in pan of hot water. Set pan in a 350° oven and bake for an hour and 15 minutes. Insert a knife into middle. If it comes out clean, pudding is done.

Yield: 4 to 6 servings

HONEY WHOLE WHEAT BREAD

Use the whole wheat setting, if your machine has one. Top the baked loaf with Honey Glaze (page 22) for extra sweetness.

REGULAR	LARGE
1½ cups bread flour	2 cups bread flour
¾ cup whole wheat flour	1 cup whole wheat flour
1½ Tbsps honey	2 Tbsps honey
⅞ cup water	1⅛ cups water
1 Tbsp butter	1½ Tbsps butter
1 tsp salt	1½ tsps salt
1 Tbsp dry milk	1½ Tbsps dry milk
1½ tsps yeast	2 tsps yeast

Load the bread pan and bake according to the instructions for your machine.

Yield: 1 loaf

WHOLE WHEAT NUT BREAD

Prepare Honey Whole Wheat Bread as above, adding raisins and nuts. Try roasted peanuts instead of pine nuts, and soak the raisins in brandy or sherry for extra flavor. To the recipe above, add:

REGULAR	LARGE
2 Tbsps pine nuts	3 Tbsps pine nuts
¼ cup raisins	⅓ cup raisins

Load the bread pan and bake according to the instructions for your machine.

Yield: 1 loaf

SPICY WHOLE WHEAT BREAD

This is a bit of delicious madness. Top with Honey Glaze after baking, while the loaf is cooling. Serve it with cream cheese and apricot preserves.

REGULAR	LARGE
1½ cups bread flour	2 cups bread flour
½ cup whole wheat flour	1 cup whole wheat flour
2 Tbsps honey	3 Tbsps honey
⅞ cup orange juice	1⅛ cups orange juice
1 Tbsp grated orange peel	1 Tbsp + 1 tsp grated orange peel
1 Tbsp butter	
1 Tbsp dry milk	1½ Tbsps butter
½ tsp anise seeds	1½ Tbsps dry milk
1 tsp salt	1 tsp anise seeds
2 tsps yeast	1½ tsps salt
	2½ tsps yeast

Load the bread pan and bake according to the instructions for your machine.

Yield: 1 loaf

HONEY GLAZE

Combine all ingredients and spread on loaf of bread as it cools.

½ cup confectioners sugar

¼ cup chopped pecans

1½ Tbsps milk

½ Tbsp honey

Yield: glaze for one loaf

LIGHT RYE BREAD

Whether your breadmaker has a rye setting or not, you will find that it does quite a good job at making rye bread. Rye flour doesn't have much gluten so it doesn't rise well. That's why there is so much white flour. Adjust the amount of caraway and proportion of rye flour to your own taste.

REGULAR	LARGE
1¾ cups bread flour	2¼ cups bread flour
½ cup rye flour	¾ cup rye flour
1 Tbsp brown sugar	1½ Tbsps brown sugar
1 tsp salt	1½ tsps salt
¾ cup water	1⅛ cups water
1 egg	1 egg
1½ tsps caraway seeds	2 tsps caraway seeds
1 Tbsp cooking oil	1½ Tbsps cooking oil
1½ tsps yeast	2 tsps yeast

Load the bread pan and bake according to the instructions for your machine.

Yield: 1 loaf

ONION RYE BREAD

Prepare Light Rye Bread as above, adding:

REGULAR	LARGE
2 Tbsps dried onions	3 Tbsps dried onions
1½ Tbsps butter (**omit oil**)	2 Tbsps butter (**omit oil**)
½ tsp black pepper	¾ tsp black pepper

Load the bread pan and bake according to the instructions for your machine.

Yield: 1 loaf

DARK RYE BREAD

Toasted bread crumbs give this bread extra flavor. Whirl leftover bread in a food processor to make crumbs. Spread the bread crumbs on a cookie sheet and run under the broiler just until brown. Watch carefully so they don't burn.

REGULAR	LARGE
1¾ cups bread flour	2 cups bread flour
⅓ cup whole wheat flour	½ cup whole wheat flour
⅓ cup rye flour	½ cup rye flour
⅞ cup water	1⅛ cups water
1 Tbsp molasses	1½ Tbsps molasses
1 Tbsp caraway seeds	1½ Tbsps caraway seeds
¼ tsp ground ginger	½ tsp ground ginger
1 Tbsp lard	1½ Tbsps lard
1 tsp salt	1 tsp salt
1½ tsps yeast	2 tsps yeast
¼ cup toasted bread crumbs	⅓ cup toasted bread crumbs

Load the bread pan and bake according to the instructions for your machine.

Yield: 1 loaf

BREAD CRUMBS

Save all those bread pieces, crusts, crumbs, heels and stale rolls. Then, put all the bits and pieces in the blender and whirl them into bread crumbs. Store in a jar.

PUMPERNICKEL BREAD

Remember the Reuben sandwich? This is the bread to use. Spread sliced bread with thousand island dressing, pile on corned beef slices, Swiss or gruyere cheese, sauerkraut, and grill in butter or olive oil. Serve with French fries, cole slaw and dark beer.

REGULAR	LARGE
1¼ cups bread flour	1¾ cups bread flour
½ cup rye flour	¾ cup rye flour
½ cup whole wheat flour	½ cup whole wheat flour
⅞ cup brewed coffee	1⅛ cups brewed coffee
1 tsp salt	1 tsp salt
1½ tsps lard	2 tsps lard
1½ tbsps cocoa	2 Tbsps cocoa
¼ cup cornmeal	⅓ cup cornmeal
2 Tbsps molasses	2½ Tbsps molasses
1 Tbsp caraway seeds	1½ Tbsps caraway seeds
¼ cup toasted bread crumbs	⅓ cup toasted bread crumbs
2 tsps yeast	2½ tsps yeast

Load the bread pan and bake according to the instructions for your machine.

Yield: 1 loaf

OATMEAL BREAD

This is an honest-to-goodness health bread. If you have leftover breakfast oatmeal, you can susbtitute it for the dry variety.

REGULAR	LARGE
2 cups bread flour	2⅓ cups bread flour
¼ cup oatmeal	⅔ cup oatmeal
2 Tbsps brown sugar	3 Tbsps brown sugar
1 Tbsp dry milk	1½ Tbsps dry milk
⅞ cup water	1⅛ cups water
1 tsp salt	1½ tsps salt
1 Tbsp butter	1½ Tbsps butter
2 tsps yeast	2½ tsps yeast

Load the bread pan and bake according to the instructions for your machine.

Yield: 1 loaf

SPICY OATMEAL BREAD

Substitute these ingredients for the last 5 items in the above recipe:

REGULAR	LARGE
3 ounces milk	½ cup milk
¼ cup applesauce	⅓ cup applesauce
1 tsp salt	1½ tsps salt
1 Tbsp butter	1½ Tbsp butter
1 tsp cinnamon	1½ tsps cinnamon
2 tsps yeast	2½ tsps yeast

Load the bread pan and bake according to the instructions for your machine.

Yield: 1 loaf

ANADAMA BREAD

The story goes that the name of this bread comes from a sea captain who had the misfortune to marry a woman who couldn't bake bread. Upset, he cursed his wife saying, "Anna, damn her!" He is alleged to have taken time to teach her this recipe, which perhaps he got from another wife in another port. You can substitute graham flour for the whole wheat, if you prefer.

REGULAR

1¾ cups bread flour
½ cup cornmeal
1 Tbsp whole wheat flour
⅝ cup water
¼ cup milk
1 Tbsp molasses
1 Tbsp butter
1 tsp salt
1½ tsps yeast

LARGE

2¼ cups bread flour
⅔ cup cornmeal
1½ Tbsps whole wheat flour
1 cup water
¼ cup milk
2 Tbsps molasses
1½ Tbsps butter
1½ tsps salt
2 tsps yeast

Load the bread pan and bake according to the instructions for your machine.

Yield: 1 loaf

HIGH PROTEIN ATHLETE'S BREAD

After several seasons as parents of a high school wrestler, we learned that feeding an athlete requires imagination—and not necessarily steak and eggs every morning. Feed this to your family sports enthusiasts.

REGULAR	LARGE
1 cup bread flour	1½ cups bread flour
½ cup high gluten flour	¾ cup high gluten flour
½ cup whole wheat flour	¾ cup whole wheat flour
¼ cup soy flour	¼ cup soy flour
⅞ cup water	1⅛ cups water
2 Tbsps dry milk	3 Tbsps dry milk
1 Tbsp shortening	1½ Tbsps shortening
2 tsps wheat germ	3 tsps wheat germ
1 Tbsp honey	2 Tbsps honey
1 tsp salt	1½ tsps salt
1½ tsps yeast	2 tsps yeast

Load the bread pan and bake according to the instructions for your machine.

Yield: 1 loaf

Chapter 3

The
Savory
Breads

DILL BREAD

If the smell of baking bread is wonderful—the smell of baking savory breads is breathtaking. The aroma of the heated herbs combines with the yeast to make the most mouth-watering air freshner you could want.

REGULAR	**LARGE**
2¼ cups bread flour	3 cups bread flour
1 Tbsp dry milk	1½ Tbsps dry milk
1½ tsps sugar	2 tsps sugar
1 tsp salt	1½ tsp salt
⅜ cup water	⅝ cup water
½ cup yogurt	¾ cup yogurt
1 egg	1 egg
1 Tbsp butter	1½ Tbsps butter
1 Tbsp fresh dill	1½ Tbsps fresh dill
1½ tsps yeast	2 tsps yeast

Load the bread pan and bake according to the instructions for your machine.

Yield: 1 loaf

BLUE CHEESE SPREAD

Combine all ingredients. Serve with sliced bread.

¼ lb. blue cheese

½ cup minced black olives

¼ lb. butter, softened

¼ cup wine vinegar

4 slices cooked bacon, crumbled

Yield: ¾ cup

HERB BREAD

This bread adds an interesting depth to meals, and improves the flavor of soups and stews. Adjust the herbs to suit your taste.

REGULAR	**LARGE**
2¼ cups bread flour	3 cups bread flour
1 Tbsp dry milk	1½ Tbsps dry milk
⅞ cup water	1⅛ cups water
2 Tbsps sugar	2½ Tbsp sugar
1 tsp salt	1½ tsps salt
1 Tbsp butter	1½ Tbsps butter
2 tsps fresh minced parsley	1 Tbsp fresh minced parsley
½ tsp savory	1 tsp savory
½ tsp thyme or sage	1 tsp thyme or sage
½ tsp marjoram	1 tsp marjoram
1½ tsps yeast	2 tsps yeast

Load the bread pan and bake according to the instructions for your machine.

Yield: 1 loaf

HERB BREAD II

Prepare Herb Bread as above, substituting celery seed and sage in the amounts listed below for the herbs in the above recipe.

REGULAR	**LARGE**
1 tsp celery seeds	1½ tsps celery seeds
½ tsp sage	1 tsp sage

Load the bread pan and bake according to the instructions for your machine.

Yield: 1 loaf

CHEESE & PEPPER LOAF

Cheese enhances the taste and enriches the nutrition of this bread, making it a substantial part of any meal. Use sharp Cheddar cheese and freshly ground pepper for maximum flavor.

REGULAR	LARGE
2 cups bread flour	3 cups bread flour
⅞ cup water	1⅛ cups water
1 Tbsp butter	1½ Tbsps butter
1 Tbsp sugar	1½ Tbsps sugar
1 tsp salt	1½ tsps salt
½ tsp basil	1 tsp basil
½ tsp black pepper	1 tsp black pepper
½ cup grated Cheddar cheese	¾ cup grated Cheddar cheese
1½ tsps yeast	2 tsps yeast

Load the bread pan and bake according to the instructions for your machine.

Yield: 1 loaf

Optional Additions: For extra zest, add one, two or all of the following:

1 Tbsp Worcestershire Sauce

¼ tsp cayenne pepper

½ tsp dry mustard

1 tsp Jaine's Crazy Mixed-Up Salt®.

THREE CHEESE BREAD

Try this feast in a loaf. If you have bits and pieces of ham, pepperoni, bologna, summer sausage or various kinds of dry cheese, mince them up and toss into the pan, too.

REGULAR	LARGE
2 cups bread flour	3 cups bread flour
½ cup yogurt	¾ cup yogurt
⅜ cup water	½ cup water
1 Tbsp sugar	1½ Tbsps sugar
1 tsp salt	1½ tsps salt
½ tsp dry mustard	¾ tsp dry mustard
1 Tbsp butter	1½ Tbsps butter
1 Tbsp crumbled blue cheese	1½ Tbsps blue cheese
1 Tbsp parmesan cheese	1½ Tbsps parmesan cheese
½ tsp black pepper	¾ tsp black pepper
½ cup grated Cheddar cheese	¾ cup grated Cheddar cheese
1½ tsps yeast	2 tsps yeast

Load the bread pan and bake according to the instructions for your machine.

Yield: 1 loaf

Optional Additions: For extra zest, add one, two or all of the following:

1 Tbsp Worcestershire Sauce
¼ tsp cayenne pepper
½ tsp dry mustard
1 tsp Jaine's Crazy Mixed-Up Salt®.

POTATO BREAD

When you make mashed potatoes, save a cup of the water used for boiling the potatoes, plus any leftover mashed potatoes. These are the secret ingredients in our family's favorite bread. (Or, substitute two tablespoons instant mashed potatoes and plain water.) Add the potato with rest of the liquids.

REGULAR	LARGE
2 cups bread flour	3 cups bread flour
⅞ cup potato water	1⅛ cups potato water
1½ Tbsps sugar	2 Tbsps sugar
1 Tbsp dry milk	1½ Tbsps dry milk
1 tsp salt	1½ tsps salt
2 Tbsps mashed potatoes	¼ cup mashed potatoes
1 Tbsp butter	2 Tbsps butter
1½ tsps yeast	2 tsps yeast
½ tsp nutmeg, optional	½ tsp nutmeg, optional

Load the bread pan and bake according to the instructions for your machine.

Yield: 1 loaf

WHOLE WHEAT POTATO BREAD: Add ¼ cup whole wheat flour and substitute 1½ Tbsps honey for the sugar.

RICH POTATO BREAD: Add 2 Tbsps soy flour and 1 Tbsp wheat germ.

GARLIC POTATO BREAD: Add 1 clove pressed garlic.

POTATO & HAM BREAD: Add 3 Tbsps Dijon mustard, ½ tsp fresh ground black pepper, plus chopped onion and minced ham, to taste.

TOMATO BREAD

This bread makes a perfect platform on which to melt some mozzarella or provolone for a light lunch. If you like, add fresh basil, oregano, chives or garlic to taste, along with the other ingredients.

REGULAR	**LARGE**
2¼ cups bread flour	3 cups bread flour
¾ cup water	1⅛ cups water
1 Tbsp olive oil	1½ Tbsps olive oil
2 Tbsps tomato paste	3 Tbsps tomato paste
1 Tbsp sugar	1½ Tbsps sugar
1 tsp salt	1½ tsps salt
1½ tsps yeast	2 tsps yeast

Combine the olive oil, tomato paste and water before adding to the bread pan. Load the bread pan and bake according to the instructions for your machine.

Yield: 1 loaf

POPEYE'S SPINACH BREAD: Subtitute ½ cup of fresh or frozen chopped spinach for the tomato paste. If using frozen spinach, thaw it and squeeze out excess water with paper towels before adding to bread pan.

CARROT BREAD

Carrot bread is good plain, but try it with the Cinnamon Butter for a real taste treat.

REGULAR	LARGE
2¼ cups bread flour	3 cups bread flour
⅞ cup water	1⅛ cups water
1½ Tbsps brown sugar	2 Tbsps brown sugar
1 tsp salt	1½ tsps salt
1 Tbsp butter	1½ Tbsps butter
⅓ cup shredded carrots	½ cup shredded carrots
¼ cup wheat germ	⅓ cup wheat germ
¼ cup chopped walnuts	⅓ cup chopped walnuts
2 tsps cinnamon	3 tsps cinnamon
1½ tsps yeast	2 tsps yeast

Load the bread pan and bake according to the instructions for your machine.

Yield: 1 loaf

CINNAMON BUTTER

Combine all ingredients. Serve with sliced bread.

¼ lb. butter, softened

½ tsp ground cinnamon

2 Tbsps sifted confectioners sugar

Yield: ¾ cup

FRESH ONION BREAD

There is a Texas onion that burns your eyes, but cooks up wonderfully. Or go ahead and use the Vadalias when they come in.

REGULAR	LARGE
2¼ cups bread flour	3 cups bread flour
⅞ cup water	1⅛ cups water
1 Tbsp sugar	1½ Tbsps sugar
1 tsp salt	1½ tsps salt
½ tsp celery salt	¾ tsp celery salt
2 Tbsps butter	2½ Tbsps butter
½ cup chopped onions	¾ cup chopped onions
1½ tsps yeast	2 tsps yeast

Sauté the onions lightly in butter, then add to the water. Load the bread pan and bake according to the instructions for your machine.

Yield: 1 loaf

PARSLEY BUTTER

Combine all ingredients, mixing well. Spread on warm bread.

 ½ cup butter, softened

 ¼ cup minced fresh parsley

 2 tsps chives

 1 clove garlic, pressed or crushed

 Yield: ¾ cup

Chapter 4

Fruit & Nut
Breads

REAL RAISIN BREAD

When we first got our breadmaker, we baked raisin bread almost every day. The candied orange peel is optional.

REGULAR	LARGE
¼ cup raisins	⅓ cup raisins
2 cups bread flour	2½ cups bread flour
¼ cup whole wheat flour	½ cup whole wheat flour
⅜ cup water	½ cup water
½ cup milk	¾ cup milk
1 Tbsp brown sugar	1½ Tbsps brown sugar
1 tsp salt	1½ tsps salt
1 Tbsp butter	1½ Tbsps butter
1 tsp cinnamon	1½ tsps cinnamon
1 tsp candied orange peel	1½ tsps candied orange peel
1½ tsps yeast	2 tsps yeast

Pour boiling water over the raisins. Let stand 15 minutes. Drain well and toss with a little flour. (For extra flavor, soak raisins in brandy instead of water.) Load the bread pan and bake according to the instructions for your machine. If your machine doesn't have a raisin bread setting, add the raisins after 20 minutes so they won't get chopped up. When done, remove loaf from pan and place on a rack. While warm, glaze with Orange Glaze.

Yield: 1 loaf

ORANGE GLAZE

Combine all ingredients, using just enough orange juice to reach spreading consistency. Pour over warm bread.

¾ cup confectioners sugar

¼ cup finely chopped walnuts

2 tsps soft butter

few drops orange juice

Yield: ¾ cup

APRICOT BREAD

This is delicious with Apricot Butter, below. If you like, substitute ¼ cup chopped apricots (⅓ cup for large loaf) for the preserves.

REGULAR	LARGE
1 egg	1 egg
2 cups bread flour	2½ cups bread flour
¼ cup whole wheat flour	½ cup whole wheat flour
⅞ cup apricot nectar	1⅛ cups apricot nectar
1 Tbsp brown sugar	1½ Tbsps brown sugar
1 tsp salt	1½ tsps salt
1 Tbsp butter	1½ Tbsps butter
1 tsp cinnamon	1½ tsps cinnamon
1 tsp grated orange peel	1½ tsps grated orange peel
2 Tbsps apricot preserves	3 Tbsps apricot preserves
1½ tsps yeast	2 tsps yeast

Topping: apricot preserves, confectioners sugar

Beat the egg in a liquid measuring cup, fill to total ⅞ cup (1¼ cups for large loaf). Load the bread pan and bake according to the instructions for your machine.

To glaze, remove loaf from the pan immediately and place on a rack. Brush top of loaf with ¼ cup warmed apricot preserves and dust with confectionars sugar.

Yield: 1 loaf

APRICOT BUTTER

Combine all ingredients and place in a small bowl.

   1 stick butter

   2 Tbsps confectioners sugar

   2 Tbsps apricot preserves

   1 Tbsp apricot liqueur, optional

   Yield: ¾ cup

BANANA BREAD

Very ripe bananas are sweeter and perfect for cooking (they are usually cheaper, too). This bread is good with either the Orange Glaze or Vanilla Glaze. Serve it warm with a cup of espresso.

REGULAR	LARGE
1 very ripe bananna	1 very ripe bananna
1 egg	1 egg
water (see instructions)	water (see instructions)
2¼ cups bread flour	3 cups bread flour
2 Tbsps butter	3 Tbsps butter
1 Tbsp dry milk	1½ Tbsps dry milk
1 Tbsp sugar	1½ Tbsps sugar
1 tsp salt	1½ tsps salt
½ tsp cinnamon	1 tsp cinnamon
1½ tsps yeast	2 tsps yeast
1 Tbsp banana liqueur, opt.	1 Tbsp banana liqueur, opt.

Mash banana and place in measuring cup. Add egg and mix the two, then add water to bring it up to a scant ⅞ cup measure (1¼ cup for the large loaf). Load the bread pan and bake according to the instructions for your machine.

When done, remove loaf from the pan immediately and place on a rack. Brush top of loaf with Orange Glaze or Vanilla Glaze.

Yield: 1 loaf

VANILLA GLAZE

Combine all ingredients and brush on warm loaf.

½ cup confectioners sugar

2 drops vanilla extract

2 tsps milk

1 pinch salt

ORANGIEST ORANGE BREAD

This is a breakfast loaf without peer. Warning: secure the kitchen from unwanted intruders—this loaf won't last.

REGULAR	LARGE
2¼ cups bread flour	3 cups bread flour
¾ cup orange juice	1⅛ cups orange juice
1 Tbsp orange marmelade	2 Tbsps orange marmelade
1½ Tbsps sugar	2 Tbsps sugar
1 tsp salt	1½ tsps salt
1 Tbsp orange liqueur	1 Tbsp orange liqueur
2 Tbsps butter	3 Tbsps butter
1 Tbsp orange zest, divided	1½ Tbsps orange zest, divided
1½ tsps yeast	2 tsps yeast

Load the bread pan and bake according to the instructions for your machine. When done, remove loaf from the pan immediately and place on a rack to cool.

Options: Add ¼ cup raisins, ¼ tsp cinnamon and ¼ tsp ground cloves. If your machine doesn't have a raisin bread setting, add the raisins after 20 minutes so they won't get chopped up.

Yield: 1 loaf

ORANGE BUTTER

Combine all ingredients and place in small bowl.

   ½ cup butter, softened

   1 Tbsp orange marmelade

   1 Tbsp orange liqueur

   1 Tbsp confectioners sugar

   ½ tsp orange zest

   Yield: ¾ cup

DATE-NUT BREAD

The addition of nuts improves the taste of the bread, makes the crust crunchy and increases the amount of protein. You can add nuts to almost any bread recipe, but keep in mind that fruits and nuts tend to inhibit the rising of the bread.

REGULAR	LARGE
2 cups bread flour	2¾ cups bread flour
2 Tbsps whole wheat flour	3 Tbsps whole wheat flour
¼ cup bran flakes	⅓ cup bran flakes
⅞ cup water	1⅛ cups water
1 Tbsp dry milk	1½ Tbsps dry milk
1 tsp salt	1½ tsps salt
2 Tbsps brown sugar	3 Tbsps brown sugar
1½ Tbsps butter	2 Tbsps butter
¼ cup chopped walnuts	⅓ cup chopped walnuts
¼ cup chopped dates	⅓ cup chopped dates
1½ tsps yeast	2 tsps yeast

Load the bread pan and bake according to the instructions for your machine. When done, remove loaf from the pan immediately and place on a rack to cool. Glaze if desired.

Yield: 1 loaf

Chapter 5

Traditional Oven Baked Breads & Rolls

FRENCH BAGUETTES

This deliciously crusty bread won't keep, but leftover slightly stale bread is good for French toast, or bread crumbs.

REGULAR	LARGE
2¼ cups unbleached all purpose flour	3 cups unbleached all purpose flour
1 tsp salt	1½ tsps salt
⅞ cup water	1⅛ cups water
1 tsp lard or olive oil	1 tsp lard or olive oil
1 tsp yeast	1½ tsps yeast
cornmeal, for baking sheet	cornmeal, for baking sheet

Topping:
1 egg yolk beaten with 2 tsp water
sesame or poppy seeds

Load the bread pan, using the dough cycle (see page 8). If your machine doesn't have a dough mode, start on regular bake cycle and remove the dough after 1½ hours. When the beeper sounds, remove dough from the bread pan and place in a greased bowl. Cover. Let dough rest in the refrigerator for 30 minutes.

Divide the dough into two or three equal pieces, rolling each into a ball. With a rolling pin, roll each ball into an oblong about ¼ inch thick. Roll the dough up tightly into a long thin log, tapering the ends and pinching ends to seal.

Sprinkle cornmeal on a greased baking sheet or baguette pan. Place the logs on the pan, seam side down. Brush top of loaves with water. Let rise in a warm place until nearly doubled in bulk, about 50 minutes.

Preheat oven to 375°. Brush logs with the egg wash. Sprinkle with poppy or sesame seeds. With a sharp knife or razor blade, make 3-4 diagonal cuts about ¼" deep across top of the logs.

Place a pan of hot water in the bottom of the oven. Bake bread at 375° for 25-30 minutes, or until golden.

Yield: 2-3 loaves

ITALIAN BREAD

Among the things New Yorkers brag of having the "best" of is bread. Here's my version of this favorite.

REGULAR

2¼ cups unbleached flour
1 Tbsp whole wheat flour
2 tsps brown sugar
1 tsp salt
⅞ cup water
1 Tbsp olive oil
1 tsp yeast
cornmeal, for baking sheet

LARGE

3 cups unbleached flour
1 Tbsp+1 tsp whole wheat flour
1 Tbsp brown sugar
1½ tsps salt
1⅛ cups water
1½ Tbsps olive oil
1½ tsps yeast
cornmeal, for baking sheet

Topping:
1 egg beaten with 1 tbsp water, plus sesame seeds as garnish

Load the bread pan, using the dough cycle (see page 8). If your machine doesn't have a dough mode, start on regular bake cycle and remove the dough after 1½ hours. When the beeper sounds, remove the dough from the bread pan. Place in a greased bowl. Cover. Let rest in the refrigerator for 30 minutes.

Divide dough into 2-3 equal pieces, rolling each into a ball. With a rolling pin, roll each ball into an oblong about ¼ inch thick.Roll the dough up tightly into a long thin log, tapering the ends and pinching the end to seal.

Sprinkle cornmeal on a greased baking sheet. Place the logs on the pan, seam side down. Brush top of loaves with water. Let rise in a warm place until nearly doubled in bulk, about 50 minutes.

Preheat oven to 375°. Brush logs with the egg wash. Sprinkle with sesame seeds. With a sharp knife or razor blade, make 4 diagonal cuts about ¼" deep, across top of the logs. Place a pan of hot water in the bottom of the oven. Bake bread at 375° for 25-30 minutes, or until golden.
Yield: 2-3 loaves

VIENNA BREAD

This was my father's favorite. We'd sit with a fresh loaf, butter and a jar of guava jelly and not get up until we finished the loaf.

REGULAR	LARGE
2¼ cups unbleached flour	3 cups unbleached flour
1 tsp sugar	1½ tsps sugar
1 tsp salt	1½ tsps salt
⅞ cup water	1⅛ cups water
1 Tbsp shortening	1½ Tbsps shortening
1½ tsp yeast	2 tsps yeast

Topping:
cornmeal, for baking sheet
1 egg white, beaten, plus sesame seeds, as garnish

Load the bread pan, using the dough cycle (see page 8). If your machine doesn't have a dough mode, start on regular bake cycle and remove the dough after 1½ hours. When the beeper sounds, remove dough from the bread pan. Place in a greased bowl. Cover. Let rest in the refrigerator for 30 minutes.

Divide the dough into 2-3 equal pieces, rolling each into a ball. With a rolling pin, roll each ball into an oblong about ¼ inch thick. Roll the dough up tightly into a long thin log, tapering the ends and pinching the end to seal.

Sprinkle cornmeal on a greased baking sheet. Place the logs on the pan, seam side down. Brush top of loaves with water. Let rise in a warm place until nearly doubled in bulk, about 50 minutes.

Preheat oven to 375°. Brush logs with the egg wash. Sprinkle with sesame seeds. With a sharp knife or razor blade, make a cut about ¼" deep, lengthwise, along the top of the loaves .

Bake bread at 375° for 25-30 minutes, or until golden. During the last five minutes, spray water on the bread and in the oven.

Yield: 2-3 loaves

CHALLAH

This is the real thing, with that chewy texture and nearly sweet taste. Add a pinch of saffron to the water for authenticity.

REGULAR	LARGE
2¼ cups all-purpose flour	3 cups all-purpose flour
1½ Tbsp sugar	2 Tbsps sugar
1 tsp salt	1½ tsps salt
¾ cup water	1 cup plus 1 oz. water
1 Tbsp cooking oil	1½ Tbsps cooking oil
1½ tsps yeast	2 tsps yeast
1 egg	1 egg

Topping:
cornmeal, for baking sheet
1 egg yolk beaten with 1 Tbsp water
Poppy seeds, as garnish

Load the bread pan, using the dough cycle (see page 8). If your machine doesn't have a dough mode, start on regular bake cycle and remove the dough after 1½ hours. When the beeper sounds, remove dough from the bread pan. Place in a greased bowl. Cover. Let rest in the refrigerator for 30 minutes.

Place dough onto a floured surface. Knead for 1-2 minutes (see page 9). Divide dough into 3 equal pieces, rolling each into a rope about 14 to 18 inches long (ends should be skinnier than the middle). Pinch the three strands together at one end and lay the ropes out parallel. Braid loosely (it will expand), pressing ends together and tucking them under the loaf.

Sprinkle cornmeal on a greased baking sheet. Place bread on the pan. Let rise in a warm place until doubled in bulk, about 50 minutes. Preheat oven to 350°. Brush loaf with egg wash. Top with poppy seeds. Bake at 350° for 30-35 minutes, or until golden.

Yield: 1 loaf

MONKEY BREAD

We serve this interesting bread often—it's fun to eat because you can just tear bits off. Use almost any sweet or savory dough.

REGULAR	LARGE
2¼ cups bread flour	3 cups bread flour
⅞ cup water	1⅛ cups water
1 Tbsp dry milk	1½ Tbsps dry milk
1 tsp salt	1¼ tsps salt
1 Tbsp sugar	1½ Tbsps sugar
1 tsp butter or lard	1½ tsps butter or lard
1½ tsps yeast	2 tsps yeast

For Dipping: ½ cup butter (or half butter and half olive oil)

Load the bread pan, using the dough cycle (see page 8). If your machine doesn't have a dough mode, start on regular bake cycle and remove the dough after 1½ hours. When the beeper sounds, remove dough from the bread pan. Place on a lightly floured surface to rest for a few minutes. Meanwhile, melt ½ cup butter in a shallow saucepan.

Roll out the dough to ¼" thickness. Cut the dough into diamonds, squares or random shapes. Dip each piece of dough into the melted butter, and place into a greased loaf, bundt or tube pan, piling pieces on top of each other as necessary. Let rise 50 minutes, or until nearly doubled in bulk. Preheat oven to 375°. Bake bread for 30 minutes, or until golden.

Yield: 1 loaf

SWEET ROLL MONKEY BREAD: Increase sugar in dough to ¼ cup. Dip dough pieces in melted butter, then roll in a mixture of brown sugar and cinnamon. Layer dough pieces in pan with raisins and walnuts and a little extra melted butter. Bake as above.

GARLIC MONKEY BREAD: Add ½ tsp garlic powder to dough. Sauté chopped garlic in melted butter and use garlic butter for dipping. Sprinkle grated Parmesan between layers. Bake as above.

PANETTONE

This is a traditional Italian Christmas bread. If you prefer, brush the prepared loaf with an egg wash and sprinkle with sugar or colored shots before baking.

2½ cups all-purpose flour
2 tsps grated lemon rind
⅝ cup milk
2 egg yolks
2 tsp honey
1 tsp salt
4 Tbsp butter
¼ cup broken walnuts
¼ cup candied fruit
3 tsps yeast

Glaze:
½ cup sifted confectioners sugar
¼ tsp vanilla extract
2 tsps milk or orange juice

2 Tbsps butter, melted, for spreading on top before baking

Load the bread pan, using the dough cycle (see page 8). If your machine doesn't have a dough mode, start on regular bake cycle and remove the dough after 1½ hours. When the beeper sounds, remove the dough from the bread pan. Put dough in a greased bowl, cover and let rest in refrigerator for 30 minutes.

Place dough in a greased tube plan or a 10" loaf pan. Spray with a fine mist of water. Let rise in warm place for 90 minutes, or until nearly doubled in bulk.

Preheat oven to 350°. Brush loaf with 2 Tbsps melted butter. Bake for 30 minutes, or until golden. Cool on rack.

To make glaze: combine all ingredients and spread on warm bread.

Yield: 1 loaf

BANANA FOSTER BREAD

Use dark or very ripe bananas. They are sweeter and perfect for cooking.

3 cups all-purpose flour
1 Tbsp sugar
1 tsp salt
⅞ cup water
¼ cup milk
2 Tbsps butter
1 egg
½ tsp cardamon
¼ tsp cinnamon
1½ tsps yeast

Banana Foster Filling:
2 Tbsps butter
½ cup brown sugar
1 Tbsp banana liqueur
1 banana

Load the bread pan, using the dough cycle (see page 8). If your machine doesn't have a dough mode, start on regular bake cycle and remove the dough after 1½ hours. When the beeper sounds, remove the dough from the bread pan. Place the dough in a greased bowl. Cover. Let rest in the refrigerator for 30 minutes.

Place dough onto a floured surface. Roll out the dough to a thin oblong about 12 to 16 inches.

To make filling: melt butter in a saucepan, add the brown sugar and liqueur, and cook over medium heat to a nice syrup. Thinly slice the banana lengthwise. Add sliced banana to syrup and cook 2-3 minutes more, stirring gently.

Spread the Banana Foster Filling over the dough. Roll it into a log and place in a 10" loaf pan, seam side down. Let rise in a warm place, about an hour.

Preheat oven to 375°. Bake bread for 30-40 minutes, or until golden. Serve hot.

Yield: 1 loaf

ROLLED RAISIN LOAF

This special occasion raisin bread is worth the effort involved.

Dough:

3 cups all-purpose flour
1½ Tbsps sugar
1 tsp salt
¼ cup water
¾ cup milk
2 Tbsps butter
1 egg
1½ tsps yeast

Filling:

½ cup water
½ cup raisins
¼ cup brandy or liqueur
½ cup brown sugar
1 tsp cinnamon
¼ tsp ground nutmeg
¼ tsp ground cloves
½ stick butter, softened

Glaze:

½ cup confectioners sugar
2 tsps milk
2 drops vanilla
1 pinch salt

Load the bread pan, using the dough cycle (see page 8). If your machine doesn't have a dough mode, start on regular bake cycle and remove the dough after 1½ hours.

When the beeper sounds, remove dough from the bread pan. Place in a greased bowl. Cover. Let dough rest in the refrigerator for 30 minutes.

For the filling, pour ½ cup boiling water over raisins. Add ½ cup brandy or liqueur. Soak for 30 minutes.

Place dough onto a floured surface. Roll out the dough into a thin oblong about 10 to 15 inches.

To fill the bread: Drain raisins and set aside. Combine sugar and spices in a small bowl. Spread softened butter over the dough. Top with an even layer of the sugar-spice mixture. Sprinkle with raisins. Tightly roll dough into a log and pinch seam to seal. Place on a greased baking sheet. Let rise in a warm place, about an hour.

Preheat oven to 350°. Bake bread for 30-40 minutes, or until golden. Combine glaze ingredients and spread over warm loaf.

Yield: 1 loaf

STOLLEN

Put joy in your home with this Christmas bread. The stollen should be kept for 2-3 days to allow the flavors to mellow.

Dough:
2 cups all-purpose flour
2 Tbsps dry milk
2 Tbsps sugar
½ tsp salt
⅝ cup water
3 Tbsps butter
1 Tbsp shortening
2 tsps yeast
1 egg
⅛ tsp mace
⅛ tsp cardamom
½ cup candied fruits
½ tsp grated lemon peel
3 Tbsps chopped pecans

Filling:
¼ cup melted butter
¼ tsp cinnamon
1 Tbsp sugar

Glaze:
½ cup confectioners sugar
1½ tsps milk
2 Tbsps melted butter

Garnish:
Sliced candied cherries
Slivered almonds

1 egg beaten, for egg wash

Load bread pan, using the dough cycle (see page 8). If machine doesn't have a dough mode, start on bake cycle and remove dough after 1½ hours. When beeper sounds, remove dough from the bread pan. Place in greased bowl. Cover. Let dough rest in refrigerator for 30 minutes. On a floured surface, roll out the dough into a 9"x 15" oval.

Filling: Brush dough with melted butter. Combine sugar and cinnamon; sprinkle over dough. Fold dough in half lengthwise and lift onto greased baking sheet. Curve ends together into a crescent shape, pressing along folded side to help the loaf keep its shape. Sprinkle dough with water. Let rise until double, about an hour.

Preheat oven to 360°. Brush stollen with a beaten egg. Bake 30-35 minutes, or until golden. Combine glaze ingredients and spread over warm loaf. Decorate with almonds and candied cherries.

Yield: 1 loaf

Chapter 6

Rolls &
Breadsticks
(Pizza, too)

HAMBURGER, HOT DOG OR DINNER ROLLS

You can shape these as simple round rolls, braid them, turn them into cloverleaf rolls, or shape hotdog or hamburger buns.

REGULAR

2¼ cups bread flour
½ cup milk
⅜ cup water
1 tsp salt
1 Tbsp sugar
1 Tbsp butter
1½ tsps yeast

LARGE

3 cups bread flour
½ cup milk
¾ cup water
1½ tsps salt
1½ Tbsps sugar
1½ Tbsps butter
2 tsps yeast

Topping:

1 egg, beaten, plus poppy or sesame seeds (optional)

Load the bread pan, using the dough cycle (see page 8). If your machine doesn't have a dough mode, start on regular bake cycle and remove dough after 1½ hours. When beeper sounds, remove dough and place in a greased bowl. Cover and let rest in refrigerator for 20 minutes. Place dough on a floured surface.

Hamburger or hot dog buns: divide dough into 8 to 12 equal pieces; shape into circles or oblongs. Put on greased baking sheet.

Cloverleaf rolls: Roll dough into a long rope and cut into equal pieces 2" long. Put 3 pieces into each section of greased muffin tin.

Mini-braids: Roll dough into a rope and cut into pieces 6" long. Braid three pieces together, tucking under ends, and place braided rolls on a greased baking sheet.

Mist shaped dough with water and let rise for 60 minutes, or until doubled in bulk. Preheat oven to 350°. Brush tops with beaten egg; sprinkle with poppy or sesame seeds. Or, brush tops of rolls with melted butter. Bake 10 to 15 minutes or until golden brown. Let hamburger or hot dog rolls cool before slicing.

Yield: 8 to 12 hamburger, hotdog or dinner rolls

CROISSANTS

A favorite of many—don't let the long directions put you off!

¾ cup milk

1 Tbsps lard

1½ Tbsps sugar

¾ tsp salt

2½ cups all-purpose flour

¼ cup water

1 tsp yeast

8 oz. tub whipped butter, softened

Heat milk in a saucepan over medium heat. Add the lard, sugar and salt. Stir and let dissolve in the pan. Let mixture cool. Dissolve yeast in 80° water. Add to milk mixture

Place milk mixture in the bread pan. Add flour. Use the dough cycle (see page 8). If your machine doesn't have a dough mode, start on regular bake cycle and remove dough after 1½ hours. When beeper sounds, remove dough and place in a greased bowl. Cover and let rest in refrigerator for an hour.

Place dough on floured surface. Roll out into a 10" x 15" rectangle, ¼" thick. Spread whipped butter over two-thirds of the rectangle. Fold the dough into thirds as follows: fold unbuttered third toward the center; fold buttered third over the unbuttered third. You should now have three layers. Repeat this step three more times. If the dough gets hard to work, let rest 5 minutes. After buttering and rolling dough 4 times, place in refrigerator to rest for 30 minutes.

Roll chilled dough into a long narrow rectangle, 6" x 16". Trim off rounded edges. Cut into 3 squares. Cut squares diagonally to make 6 triangles. Roll triangles out and shape into crescents.

Place rolls on greased baking sheets and chill 30 minutes. Preheat oven to 400°. Brush rolls with butter. Bake at 400° for 10 minutes. Reduce heat to 350° and bake 10 to 15 minutes, or until golden.

Yield: 6 croissants

BREADSTICKS

A necessity with soup, stew or chowder. Make them fat, thin, long, short, crisp or chewy, as you like.

2¼ cups bread flour
¼ cup milk
⅝ cup water
1 tsp butter
1 Tbsp sugar
1 tsp salt
1½ tsps yeast

Toppings:
1 egg white, beaten
poppy seeds, optional
sesame seeds, optional
coarse salt, optional

Load the bread pan, using the dough cycle (see page 8). If your machine doesn't have a dough mode, start on regular bake cycle and remove dough after 1½ hours. When beeper sounds, remove dough and place in a greased bowl. Cover and let rest in refrigerator for 20 minutes. Place dough on a floured surface.

Divide dough into four or five pieces. Roll each piece into a long rope. Cut ropes into long or short breadsticks and place on greased baking sheets.

Mist shaped dough with water and let rise in a warm place for 30 minutes, or until doubled in bulk. Preheat oven to 350°.

Brush breadsticks with beaten egg white; sprinkle with poppy seeds, seasame seeds or coarse salt. Bake at 350° for 10 to 15 minutes, or until golden brown. (Bake 20 minutes for crispy breadsticks.) Remove from pans to cool.

Yield: about 24 breadsticks

ENGLISH MUFFINS

These are as good as the best you can buy. Make the dough the night before and bake in the morning. Serve with butter and jam.

½ cup milk	2¼ cups bread flour
1½ Tbsps butter	1 Tbsp sugar
cold water (see below)	1 tsp salt
1½ tsps cider vinegar	1 tsp yeast
1 egg, beaten	1 cup cornmeal, as coating
	cooking oil, for frying

Warm the milk in a saucepan. Add butter, stirring to melt. Add the slightly beaten egg. Combine enough cold water and vinegar to equal ⅜ cup, and add to milk mixture. Place liquid in bread pan, then flour, sugar and salt. Add yeast last. (For bread makers with a separate yeast dispenser, add yeast to dispenser as directed.)

Use the dough cycle (see page 8). If your machine doesn't have a dough mode, start on regular bake cycle and remove dough after 1½ hours. When beeper sounds, remove dough and place in a greased bowl. Cover with plastic wrap and let rest in refrigerator for 30 minutes (or overnight if you plan bake the next day).

Put cornmeal in a bowl. Shape ½ cup of dough into a round ball. Roll the ball in corn meal. Flatten ball into a circle that is ½" thick and about 4" round. Repeat with remaining dough. Let prepared muffins rise in a warm place about 10 minutes.

Heat 2 tablespoons cooking oil in a skillet. Cook the muffins, 3 to 4 at a time, covered, for 6 minutes per side. Check often to make sure they are not browning too quickly. Remove muffins from pan and place on paper towels.

Using a fork, split the muffins apart. Toast and serve hot.

Yield: 8 muffins

HOT CROSS BUNS

These are quintessentially English and not terribly sweet. They are usually served on Sundays during lent.

2½ cups all purpose flour
¾ cup water
¼ cup milk
1 egg
⅓ cup raisins, plumped
¼ cup candied citrus rind
½ tsp salt
¼ tsp cinnamon
2 Tbsps butter
½ tsp cardamom
1 Tbsp sugar
1 tsp yeast

1 beaten egg, for egg wash

Frosting:
1 cup confectioners sugar
1 Tbsp milk
¼ tsp vanilla extract

Load bread pan, using dough cycle (see page 8). If your machine doesn't have a dough mode, start on regular bake cycle and remove dough after 1½ hours. When beeper sounds, remove dough and place in greased bowl. Cover with plastic wrap and let rest in refrigerator for 30 minutes. On a lightly floured surface, knead the raisins and candied citrus rind into the dough.

Divide dough into 9 equal pieces and shape each into a bun. Place the buns into a baking pan in three rows of three. Let rise in a warm place, covered, for 45 minutes.

Brush tops with egg wash and bake for 20 to 25 minutes in a 350° oven, or until buns are beautifully browned. Remove buns from the pan and set on a cooling rack.

Frosting: Combine confectioners sugar, milk and vanilla extract, beating until smooth. Add more sugar or milk as necessary to make the frosting of good piping consistency. Place the frosting into a small pastry bag and pipe a cross on the top of each cooled bun. (Or, put the frosting into a small plastic bag, cut off one corner and pipe frosting onto buns.)

Yield: 9 buns

DANISH PASTRIES

This is one of our favorite recipes.

Ingredients:
2¼ cups all purpose flour
⅞ cup milk
4 Tbsps butter
1 egg, beaten, for brushing on top
2 Tbsps sugar
½ tsp salt
2 tsps yeast

1½ Tbsps sugar
½ tsp cinnamon

Filling:
3 oz. cream cheese
1½ Tbsps sugar
½ Tbsp lemon juice
1 tsp beaten egg
¼ tsp vanilla

Frosting:
½ cup confectioners sugar
1 Tbsp milk
⅛ tsp vanilla extract

Load bread pan, using dough cycle (see page 8). If your machine doesn't have a dough mode, start on regular bake cycle and remove dough after 1½ hours. When beeper sounds, remove dough and place in greased bowl. Cover with plastic wrap and let rest in refrigerator for 30 minutes.

On a lightly floured surface, roll out the dough into a 12" x 15" rectangle. Combine sugar and cinnamon; sprinkle over top. Roll dough up jelly roll fashion into a 12" log. Brush seam with beaten egg. Slice log into 12 one-inch pieces. Place rolls on two greased cookie sheets, not touching. Mist with water. Let rise in a warm place for 30 minutes, or until doubled.

Filling: Combine softened cream cheese with sugar. Gradually add the lemon juice, egg and vanilla. Enlarge the hole in the center of each bun and drop in 2 Tbsps of filling. Brush rolls with remaining beaten egg. Bake in a preheated 360°. oven for 10 to 15 minutes, or until golden brown. Place on rack to cool.

Frosting: Combine confectioners sugar, milk and vanilla extract, beating until smooth. Drizzle from a spoon to decorate the tops of the Danishes.

Yield: 12 Danishes

Try either of these fillings for a delicious variation on the basic Danish pastry.

Butterscotch Apple Filling
This makes enough filling for 16 pastries.

2 apples
6 Tbsps brown sugar
2 Tbsps butter
½ tsp cinnamon

Peel and thinly slice the apples. Melt the butter in a small frying pan over medium heat.

Add the pieces of apple, the brown sugar and cinnamon. Sauté about 5 to 7 minutes, or until done. Cool mixture. Fill pastries with the apple filling and bake as directed.

Cherry Filling
This makes enough filling for 24 pastries.

1 No. 2 can pitted sour cherries
2 Tbsps cornstarch
½ cup sugar
½ tsp cinnamon, optional
⅛ tsp salt

Drain cherries, reserving the juice. Set aside.

In a medium saucepan, combine the sugar, cinnamon, salt and cornstarch. Gradually add the reserved cherry juice. Bring to a boil over medium high heat. Cook until thickened and clear.

Stir in cherries. Cool mixture. Fill pastries with the cherry filling and bake as directed.

CINNAMON BUNS

Here's the recipe for that perennial sweet-tooth favorite.

2½ cups all purpose flour
¾ cup milk
1 egg plus water to = ¼ cup
2 Tbsps butter
2 Tbsps sugar
1 tsp salt
1 tsp cinnamon
1½ tsps yeast

1 egg, beaten, for egg wash

Filling:
1 tsp cinnamon
2 Tbsps brown sugar
2 Tbsps melted butter
¼ cup chopped raisins

Frosting:
1 cup confectioners sugar
1 Tbsp milk
¼ tsp vanilla extract

Load bread pan, using dough cycle (see page 8). If your machine doesn't have a dough mode, start on regular bake cycle and remove dough after 1½ hours. When beeper sounds, remove dough and place in greased bowl. Cover with plastic wrap and let rest in refrigerator for 30 minutes. On a lightly floured surface, roll out the dough into a 10" x 16" rectangle.

Filling: Brush dough with melted butter. Combine cinnamon and sugar; sprinkle over top. Scatter raisins over dough. Roll dough up jelly roll fashion into a 16" log. Brush seam with beaten egg. Slice log into 12 pieces. Place buns in a 9" x 13" pan, not touching. Mist with water. Let rise in a warm place for 30 minutes, or until doubled. Brush buns with beaten egg. Preheat oven to 360°. Bake 15 to 20 minutes, or until golden. Place on rack to cool.

Frosting: Combine confectioners sugar, milk and vanilla extract, beating until smooth. Spread over warm cinnamon buns.

STICKY BUNS: Prepare **Cinnamon Buns** as directed above through slicing the rolled dough. In a 9" x 13" baking pan, combine 2 tbsps melted butter, ½ cup brown sugar and ¼ cup chopped walnuts. Place sliced dough in pan, on top of butter-sugar mixture. Follow recipe above for rising and baking. After baking, remove pan from oven and invert onto a large platter. Scrape any extra syrup or nuts out of pan and drizzle over the sticky buns.

Yield: 12 rolls

ROB & HOLLY'S PIZZA

We think our homemade pizza surpasses any delivered variety.

REGULAR

2¼ cups flour
⅞ cup water
1 tsp salt
1 Tbsp olive oil
1 tsp yeast

LARGE

3 cups flour
1⅛ cups water
1¼ tsps salt
1½ Tbsps olive oil
1½ tsps yeast

Toppings:
Cornmeal for preparing pans, pizza sauce, grated parmesan cheese, shredded mozzarella, pepperoni, sausage, anchovies, mushrooms, onions, green peppers, or other favorites.

Load the bread pan, using the dough cycle (see page 8). If your machine doesn't have a dough mode, start on regular bake cycle and remove dough after 1½ hours. When beeper sounds, remove dough. Let rest 5 minutes. Divide dough into 2 or 3 pieces. Roll each piece into a ball. Flatten and stretch the dough from the center until each piece is large enough to fill pizza pan. Preheat oven to 400°. Grease pizza pans and sprinkle with cornmeal. Place dough on pans. Prick surface with a fork. Sprinkle with parmesan cheese. Spread with pizza sauce. Top with mozzarella and favorite pizza toppings. Bake at 400° for 15 to 20 minutes.

Yield: 2 large or 3 small pizzas

WHITE PIZZA: Sauté ½ cup chopped onion with 3 chopped cloves garlic in 2 Tbsps olive oil. When tender, add 2 Tbsps melted butter. Add onion mixture to 1 cup ricotta cheese. Spread on pizza crust, cover with mozzarella. Bake at 400° for 15 minutes.

STROMBOLI: Roll dough into an oblong, ¼" thick. Spread with pizza sauce. Top with pepperoni, mozzarella, sautéed onions, mushrooms, etc. Roll tightly. Bake at 400° for about 25 minutes.

EASY PIZZA SAUCE: In 1 Tbsp olive oil, sauté 2 chopped cloves garlic, 1 tsp dried basil and ½ tsp oregano, just until fragrant. Add one 6-ounce can tomato paste and ¼ cup water. Heat to boiling.

HAWAIIAN BREAKFAST PIZZA

The perfect way to start the day for people who prefer to eat nothing but pizza. Or, you can serve this as an unusual dessert!

DOUGH
¼ cup milk
1 cup water
3 cups all-purpose flour
3 Tbsps sugar
2 Tbsps butter
1 tsp salt
1½ tsps yeast

TOPPING
1 cup brown sugar
1 16-oz. can crushed pineapple
¼ cup butter

Load the bread pan, using the dough cycle (see page 8). If your machine doesn't have a dough mode, start on regular bake cycle and remove dough after 1½ hours. When beeper sounds, remove dough. Place the dough in a greased bowl. Cover. Rest the dough in the refrigerator for 30 minutes (or overnight).

Divide dough into 2 or 3 pieces. Roll each piece into a ball. Flatten and stretch the dough from the center out until each piece is large enough to fill your pizza pans. Preheat oven to 400°.

Topping: Drain the crushed pineapple, reserving juice. In a medium saucepan over medium heat, melt ¼ cup butter. Stir in brown sugar and ¼ cup pineapple juice. Cook until thickened, stirring frequently.

Grease pizza pans and sprinkle each pan with a Tbsp of cornmeal. Place dough on pans. Prick surface with a fork.

Spread dough with brown sugar sauce, then top evenly with the drained crushed pineapple. Cover with foil and bake at 400° for 10 minutes, then bake another 5 to 7 minutes uncovered. Serve hot.

Yield: 2 large or 3 small pizzas